Whispers for a Magical Time

Words by
jani johe webster

Photographs by
Suzanne Webb

Suzanne Webb

Text ©2008 by jani johe webster
Photograph ©2008 by Suzanne Webb

Cover photograph by Suzanne Webb

Book design by Craig Grant & Grant Associates

Library of Congress Control Number: 2008905894

ISBN-13: 9780961829261

ISBN-10: 0961829265

StarMist Books
Box 12640
Rochester, NY 14612

starmistbooks@comcast.net

"time pretending": reprinted from a *spider on the wall* ©1983 by jani johe webster

time pretending

where did it go
when we weren't looking
time pretending to be other things –

a snowflake melting
as it falls...
a cobweb dangling
from a tree...
rose petals dropping
from a summer vase...

winter seagulls

the first day
of the new year

turning to look
i see with wonder
two seagulls
circling
white in a deep
        blue sky

an omen
of blessings

send a poem

thru
the snowflakes
of
dawn

i am
walking
into
a
poem
tonite

from a
distance

spring
beckons

bells ring out
with the music
of spring

whispers for a
magical time

my dreams
laugh quietly
in a tiger lily field

meet my hopes
as they come walking

thru a dew covered
morn

traveling now
over the horizon

to find the footprint
of my muse

there is a
shimmering blue light

messages

leaves of summer
in a warm wind

messages of green
whisper in a

waiting

world

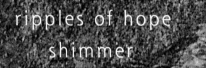

ripples of hope
shimmer

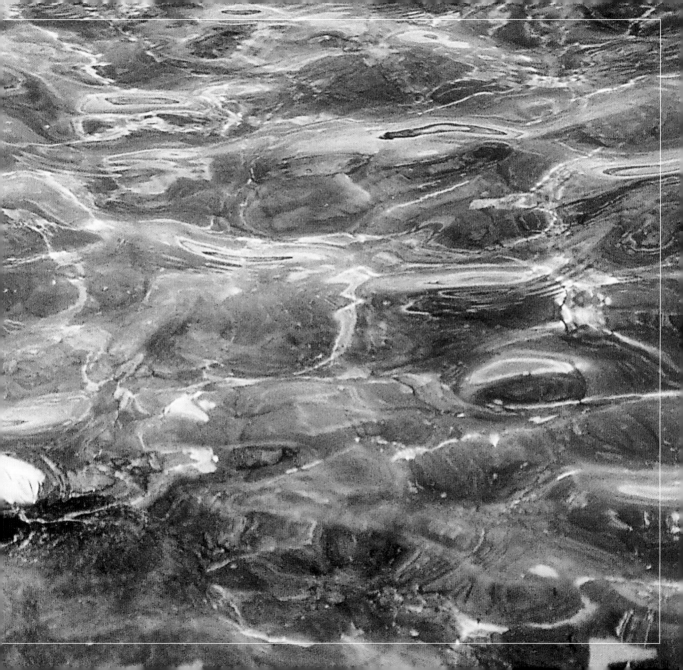

the minutes move
on the hinges of time

and the curtains of
magic open

blue

i feel
blue
touching me
softly

clouds moving

did you see how the sky
was streaked at sunset
did you listen to the
singing of the shells
could you hear the sound
of the clouds moving
and know the ending
of this day

autumn search

falling leaves of autumn
crimson and gold
on an emerald screen

october haze
as misty as a dream
and early morning flight
of far-off geese

edge of the sky

i am writing tonight
on the edge of the sky
and between the moon
and the sun

now
an autumn
night
approaches

searching
for
its
moon

autumn gold

the sun spilled gold
through autumn leaves
and all the earth
gathered it

storing
for when
    the winter
       came

song of sleep

dusk approached
the darkness
singing day
to sleep

sometimes

did you think sometimes
you were something else
like a mocking bird
or a weeping willow

did you walk sometimes
going backwards
or light candles
in the middle of the day

let's go then
where no ship has ever sailed
and spend our lives with falling stars
until we can spend
no   more

jani johe webster is the author of three collections of poetry: *a spider on the wall, sound of a shadow,* and *silhouette of a soul,* as well as a chapbook, *from a distance.* For the past three decades, her poetry has appeared in literary and international anthologies and periodicals, including *Amherst Society, The Hayden Poetry Review,* and *Up Against the Wall Mother.* She is the recipient of a number of awards, including the Calliope Scintillations Contest. She has co-authored two picture books with her daughter, Nila J. Webster: *Remember Rain and Songs of Wonder for the Night Sea Journey,* and *Remember Beauty and Songs for a Blue Time.*

Suzanne Webb resides in the historic seaport city of Salem, Massachusetts. For over twenty-five years, she has been an elementary school teacher, dedicating her energy to the art of teaching and to helping children develop confidence in every discipline. In her magical and child-centered classroom, poetry and photography are presented as special ways of communicating and connecting. The study of poetry and photography are highlights of learning throughout the school year, bringing life's beauty into the classroom and lives of the students. *Whispers for a Magical Time* is her first book. She has two beautiful daughters, Samantha and Emily.